"This book made me nervous whe[n] through it because I knew it would w..... self-help book; it's more of a blue-collar, get-down-to-business friend with calloused hands who is ready to boogie when you are. This book is about action, but also acknowledgment. There are no platitudes and its author is no Pollyanna. It's an explicit map that leads to a place where you're going to feel measurably better, and better equipped to face life's vicissitudes."

ROB DELANEY, COMEDIAN

"This book does the work that I believe is most worthwhile – it does not hand you answers; it sets you up to find them yourself. One of the most accessible, relatable, unique, and flawlessly crafted books that I have ever seen. A must-have, a must-read, a must-do."

Brianna Wiest, author of *The Human Element*

"Taking the small incremental steps toward conquering depression takes courage, and even then, it helps to have any compassionate guidance you can find. *How to Be Happy (Or at Least Less Sad)* comes from a knowing, forgiving place. Its intentions are sincere. When I first read it I thought: I could have used a book like this. And then I thought: I still can use a book like this."

JASON PORTER, AUTHOR OF *WHY ARE YOU SO SAD?*

"This book is the kind of friend I want around when I'm feeling sad. He lets me vent without judging me, gives me a little guidance, reminds me that I'm not alone, and lets me draw all over him with colored pencils."

Lisa Currie, author of *The Scribble Diary* and *Me, You, Us*

"Whether you are just having a random sad day, or your bad days come a little bit more frequently than that, this book will help you shine a new light on your life. Filled with thoughtful, simple, and heart-opening exercises, plus snippets and stories from the author's own struggles, this book will give you a new lens that will help you get through the rough patches, week by week, day by day, or minute by minute if that's all you can handle.

Fill out these pages. You'll laugh. You'll cry. And you'll be blown away by what you discover about your own ability to feel happy. Or at least less sad."

BERNADETTE NOLL, AUTHOR OF *SLOW FAMILY LIVING*

~~CHEER UP~~

~~IT'S ALL IN YOUR HEAD~~

~~THINK HAPPY THOUGHTS~~

~~PULL YOURSELF TOGETHER~~

~~WHAT'S YOUR PROBLEM?~~

~~SNAP OUT OF IT~~

HOW TO BE HAPPY
(OR AT LEAST LESS SAD)

LEE CRUTCHLEY

A PERIGEE BOOK

A PERIGEE BOOK

An imprint of Penguin Random House LLC
New York, New York 10019

PENGUIN.com

A Penguin Random House Company

HOW TO BE HAPPY (OR AT LEAST LESS SAD)

Proprietary ISBN: 9781101949030

PRINTED IN THE UNITED STATES OF AMERICA

10   9   8   7

FOR Indi May

A CONSTANT BRIGHT LIGHT
IN A SOMETIMES DARK WORLD.

I HOPE YOU NEVER NEED THIS BOOK.

FOREWORD

The problem with a lot of advice about how to be happy is that it's rubbish: unadulterated, weapons-grade nonsense. A few examples: If you're like most people, research suggests, you won't make your dreams come true by thinking positive, searching for your life purpose, or saying "I'm a winner!" to your reflection in the bathroom mirror every morning. Another problem with happiness advice is that the good bits – the parts that actually do work – sound as if they don't. They come wrapped in New Agey language, or from the kind of shifty guru you wouldn't trust to feed your cat while you went on holiday. Oh, and just to make matters worse, trying too hard to be happy will make you miserable, so even the best advice can backfire. To be honest, you'd be forgiven for just giving up.

You shouldn't, though. Instead, you should grab a pencil and start filling in the blanks and answering the questions in this book. For one thing, Lee Crutchley isn't a self-help guru with a deeply unsettling smile; he's not going to tell you to place your trust in The Universe or eliminate the word "impossible" from your vocabulary. For another thing, the witty, practical outlook you'll find here is in line both with modern psychological research and ancient philosophical wisdom. Stop stressing yourself out trying to control the things you'll never be able to control. Rather than trying to persuade yourself that everything will be fine, consider asking what's the worst that could happen if things don't turn out fine. The more you try to avoid all suffering, the more you'll suffer. Perfection isn't achievable – and it would make you an extremely dull person if it were.

The best part, though, is that this isn't really a book of happiness advice at all. Instead, it's a tool for plumbing the depths of your own mind and dredging up your own wisdom: the stuff that you already know, deep down, but that it's all too easy to forget amid the daily whirlwind of work, family responsibilities, commuting, and catching up with online galleries of Otters Who Look Like Benedict Cumberbatch.

Science is on Lee's side, too: Again and again, psychologists have shown that writing things down transforms us in fundamental ways. (There's even some evidence that physical injuries heal faster if you spend some time writing in a journal.) They've also shown that the tiniest ways of altering your experience of the world – breathing more slowly, walking barefoot, unplugging from the web, just for a day – can lead to the biggest changes.

So I urge you to dive in. After all, what's the worst that could happen? (I mean, unless you're driving at the same time or something – don't do that.) There's a huge amount of wisdom in these pages – and there'll be even more when you've finished with it.

OLIVER BURKEMAN

HAPPY IS A

STRONG WORD

JOHN LUTHER

happy

/ˈhapi/

ADJECTIVE

1. FEELING OR SHOWING PLEASURE OR CONTENTMENT.

2. FORTUNATE AND CONVENIENT.

HELLO,

I guess you are reading this book because you feel sad and you want to feel happy. You are probably hoping this book will provide the answers to a happy and fulfilling life. You may even be hoping that I know some kind of "secret." I am sorry to say that I don't.

This book will not fix you, and it will not make you happy. There are plenty of books out there that will promise to do both of those things. There are plenty more that will promise to change your life, but how many of those have you already read? And how many worked? In my experience, the books least likely to change your life are the books that promise to do so.

I should probably say at this point that I'm not a doctor, nor do I have any qualifications in the area of mental health. I'm just a guy who gets sad sometimes, and last year I got really sad. I won't go into details, but I'm sure you can imagine the kind of really sad I'm talking about. It was the kind of really sad that is quickly replaced by emptiness, numbness, and an overwhelming sense that everything is doomed and hopeless.

I spent a lot of time thinking during that period, and I managed to figure out one of the reasons I was feeling so sad, so often. I know this might sound weird, but I realized it was partly because I was trying so very hard to BE HAPPY. The more I tried to be happy, the harder it became, and the harder it became, the sadder I felt.

I don't remember exactly how or when it happened, but one day I decided to completely give up on trying to be happy. It clearly wasn't working. I decided I would try to be a bit less sad instead, which felt so much more achievable. In fact, the working title for this book was *Have You Tried Being Less Sad?*

Even though that didn't quite work as a book title, I still think it's one of the most important questions you can ask yourself when you're spiralling into sadness.

Over the last year or so, I researched a lot about how the brain and the body work, I read a lot of different philosophical and spiritual approaches to happiness and sadness, and I read a lot about how other depressed people felt — and how they started to feel better. Along the way I tried a lot of small things in the hope that they would help me feel a bit less sad, and as a result I have been much happier. In fact, if there is any kind of secret, it's that being less sad is the same as being more happy.

This book is full of all of those things that I tried. All of the tasks are based — sometimes abstractly — on my research, experiences, and proven science. Some of them worked for me and some of them didn't, and I'm sure the same will apply to you. That's because there is no one-size-fits-all solution when it comes to feeling less sad. It's about finding things that work for you. More importantly, it's about remembering those things when you need them. Which can be harder than it sounds.

There will probably be pages of this book that you find uncomfortable, but once you get used to that, you'll see it's a good thing. There's an exercise you can try to see this in action.

Bend your fingers back to the point where they start to feel uncomfortable, and just hold them there for a while. Your first instinct will be to stop because it doesn't feel nice. But if you hold that position you'll see that those feelings quickly dissipate. You'll realize the pain isn't as bad as you first imagined, and as the pain dulls it will be replaced with warmth. When you finally let go your fingers will probably even feel a little better. Remember those feelings if you ever feel uncomfortable while working through this book, and keep going.

The most important thing about feeling less sad is that you actually have to put in some effort, no matter how small. I know that doesn't sound fun, and I know how hard that can be sometimes. There will still be days when you don't want to go outside, or talk to anyone, or even get out of bed — and this book can help you, even on those days. There is comfort when you need to wallow in sadness, a nudge when you just feel ok, and encouragement on those days when you feel at your best. But the one thing you have to promise yourself is to always try.

And while I may not know the secrets that can make you feel happy, I promise that this book can help you feel less sad.

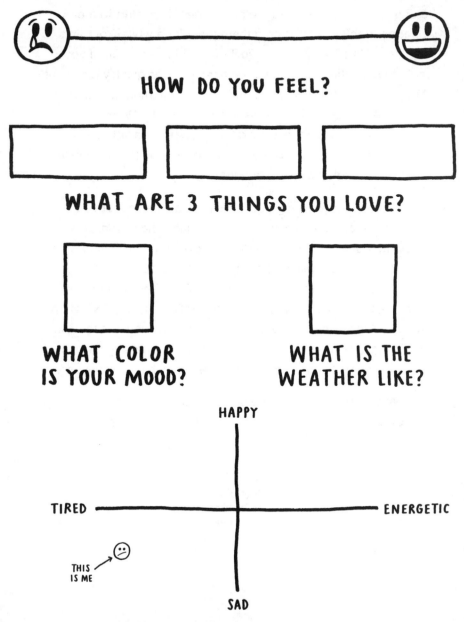

WHERE ARE YOU HEADING?

WHAT SHAPE
IS YOUR LIFE?

WHAT IS THE MOST
IMPORTANT THING?

HOW FULL IS
YOUR MIND?

HOW FULL IS
YOUR HEART?

WHEN WAS THE LAST TIME YOU WERE HAPPY?

RATE THESE AREAS OF YOUR LIFE.
ADD AN ARROW TO SHOW IF IT'S GETTING BETTER OR WORSE.

EX:

OVERALL MOOD: 1 2 3 4 5 6 7 8 9 10
FAMILY: 1 2 3 4 5 6 7 8 9 10
FRIENDS: 1 2 3 4 5 6 7 8 9 10
SOCIAL LIFE: 1 2 3 4 5 6 7 8 9 10
RELATIONSHIP: 1 2 3 4 5 6 7 8 9 10
HAVING FUN: 1 2 3 4 5 6 7 8 9 10
WORK: 1 2 3 4 5 6 7 8 9 10
MONEY: 1 2 3 4 5 6 7 8 9 10
EATING HEALTHY: 1 2 3 4 5 6 7 8 9 10
DRINKING WATER: 1 2 3 4 5 6 7 8 9 10
GOING OUTSIDE: 1 2 3 4 5 6 7 8 9 10
EXERCISE (UGH): 1 2 3 4 5 6 7 8 9 10
HEALTH: 1 2 3 4 5 6 7 8 9 10
CREATIVITY: 1 2 3 4 5 6 7 8 9 10
SENSE OF PURPOSE: 1 2 3 4 5 6 7 8 9 10
THE PAST: 1 2 3 4 5 6 7 8 9 10
THE PRESENT: 1 2 3 4 5 6 7 8 9 10
THE FUTURE: 1 2 3 4 5 6 7 8 9 10

LIST THINGS YOU DO EVERY DAY
THAT GIVE YOU NO PLEASURE

CROSS OUT ANYTHING NON-ESSENTIAL

LIST THINGS YOU DO EVERY DAY THAT GIVE YOU PLEASURE

CIRCLE ANYTHING NON-ESSENTIAL

THINK OF TEN THINGS IN YOUR LIFE THAT YOU'RE GRATEFUL FOR.
THEY COULD BE PEOPLE, PLACES, OR PIZZA.
WRITE ONE THING ON EACH FINGER OF THESE HANDS.

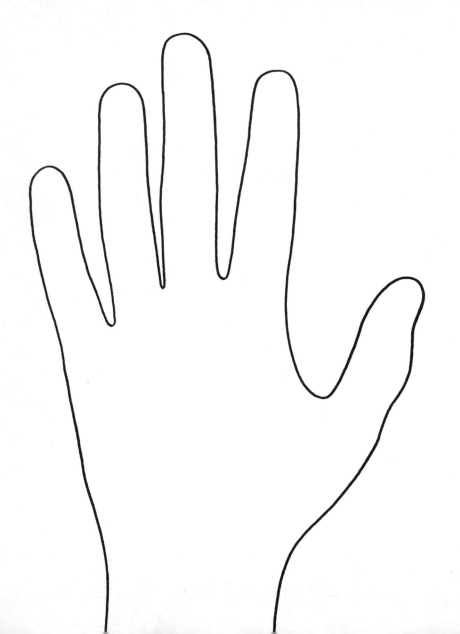

WHENEVER YOU'RE FEELING LOW,
REMEMBER THAT THESE THINGS ARE ALWAYS WITHIN REACH.
COUNT THEM OFF, THEN GO AND FIND ONE.

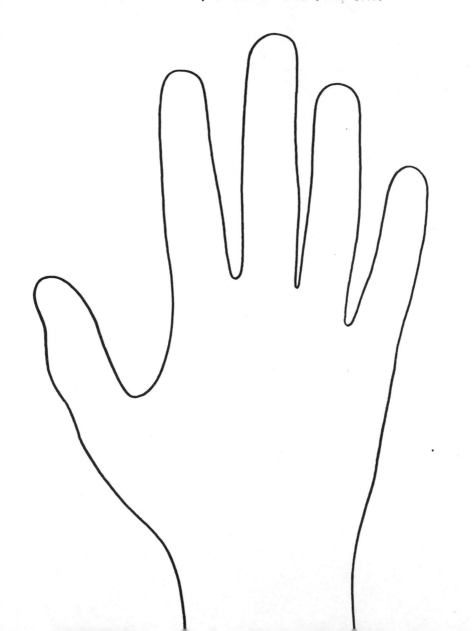

WRITE EVERYTHING BAD IN THIS BOX

WRITE EVERYTHING GOOD IN THIS BOX

THE BEST DREAM YOU CAN REMEMBER

THE WORST DREAM/NIGHTMARE

DO YOU FEEL LIKE CRYING?

☐ YES – THAT'S OK, HAVE A LITTLE CRY NOW.

☐ NO – SERIOUSLY? THAT'S COOL!
      BUT MAYBE YOU SHOULD HAVE A CRY ANYWAY?

ON THE OPPOSITE PAGE IS A LIST OF GOOD PLACES
I'VE FOUND TO CRY. FEEL FREE TO ADD YOUR OWN.

GOOD PLACES TO CRY

RAIN (TRY TO KEEP SMILING)

BED

THE SHOWER

SWIMMING POOL (UNDERWATER)

Our brains are better — and some would say faster — at processing negative information than positive. This was very useful for keeping us alive in the past, when our lives were often under threat. But it's not so useful today, when our minds are telling our brains that we are worthless idiots. Our brains tend to believe it.

A good way to combat this is to make an effort to notice the positives in each day. Our brains can actually be rewired through repetition to look for those positives with less effort on our part — the term for this is neuroplasticity.

The simple daily exercise of writing down a few positive events — no matter how small — can make a huge difference.

YOUR BRAIN IS
DESIGNED TO
KEEP YOU ALIVE.
IT DOESN'T GIVE
A SHIT ABOUT
YOUR HAPPINESS.

RUBY WAX

THINGS TO DO

KEEP A DAILY DIARY

WRITE MORE ABOUT MOODS AND THOUGHTS THAN EVENTS.
COME BACK TO THIS PAGE AND DRAW YOUR MOOD.
DOES IT IMPROVE, GET WORSE, OR FLUCTUATE?

FOR 30 DAYS

GO OUTSIDE ONCE A DAY

SPEND AT LEAST 10 MINUTES JUST BEING OUT THERE.
DRAW A SYMBOL TO REPRESENT THE WEATHER.
DOES THE WEATHER AFFECT YOUR MOOD?

LIST THE NEGATIVE THOUGHTS YOU HAVE MOST OFTEN

I HATE BEING ALONE

GIVE THEM A MORE POSITIVE SPIN

I'D LIKE TO MEET NEW PEOPLE

BREATHING IS REALLY EASY, BUT IT'S ALSO
REALLY EASY TO FORGET HOW TO DO IT PROPERLY.

A LOT OF US TAKE SHORT SHALLOW BREATHS
WITHOUT REALIZING, OR FORGET TO USE BOTH
OUR NOSE AND MOUTH.

THE KEY IS TO INHALE SLOWLY THROUGH YOUR
NOSE AND EXHALE SLOWLY THROUGH YOUR MOUTH.
IT ALSO HELPS TO EXHALE FOR SLIGHTLY LONGER.
A GOOD TRICK IS TO COUNT TO THREE AS YOU
INHALE AND FIVE AS YOU EXHALE.

BREATHING PROPERLY IS ONE OF THE BEST WAYS
TO CALM YOURSELF DOWN. TRY IT FOR A
MINUTE NEXT TIME YOU'RE FEELING ANXIOUS.

THE BEST PART IS YOU CAN DO THIS ANYWHERE!

How to Breathe

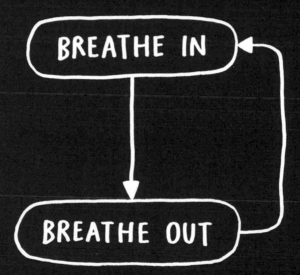

WHAT QUALITY DO YOU
THINK YOU PROJECT MOST?

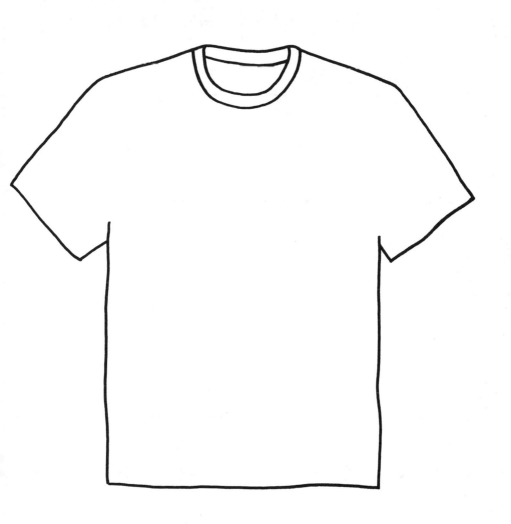

WHAT QUALITY DO YOU
WISH TO PROJECT MOST?

LIST 10 THINGS THAT MAKE YOU FEEL ANXIOUS AND RATE HOW ANXIOUS THEY MAKE YOU (1 TO 10)

MAKING LISTS

RE-ORDER THE LIST FROM LOW TO HIGH. START WORKING
THROUGH THIS LIST — DO AT LEAST ONE TASK A WEEK

~~MAKING LISTS~~ _____ __

_____ __

_____ __

_____ __

_____ __

_____ __

_____ __

_____ __

_____ __

_____ __

FILL THIS BOX WITH YOUR
BIGGEST WORRY RIGHT NOW.

IMAGINE YOUR BEST FRIEND IS WORRYING ABOUT THIS. GIVE THEM SOME ADVICE.

I always found describing my depression really hard. When you say that you're depressed, most people think it means that you just feel sad, and their instinct is to try to cheer you up. It's hard to explain that you feel completely numb, or nothing at all, or like you want to curl up into a ball so tightly that you disappear forever. People who have never felt that way cannot relate.

Depression really does limit your ability to construct a future — and not just a future where you're happy, but a future where you even get out of bed in the morning. When I am struggling to construct that future, looking to the past always helps me. I know I've felt that way before, and I know that I've come through it — it's a fact. It doesn't change the way I feel, but it does remind me that I won't feel that way forever. Which is a really good thing to remember.

DEPRESSION IS THE INABILITY TO CONSTRUCT A FUTURE

SIDE EFFECTS (2013)

DIR. STEVEN SODERBERGH [FILM]
USA: OPEN ROAD FILMS

IMAGINE SOME TIME IN THE FUTURE
WHEN YOU'RE "IN A BETTER PLACE."

YOU'RE MORE CONFIDENT ABOUT WHO YOU
ARE, WHERE YOU ARE, AND WHAT YOU WANT.

WRITE YOURSELF AN EMAIL FROM THAT FUTURE.

DO YOU NEED ENCOURAGEMENT, REASSURANCE,
OR ~~A KICK IN THE~~ A LITTLE TOUGH LOVE?

TELL YOURSELF THE THINGS YOU NEED TO KNOW.

USE FUTUREME.ORG TO SEND YOURSELF THIS
EMAIL ON A DAY YOU THINK YOU'LL NEED IT.

SUBJECT:

SEND

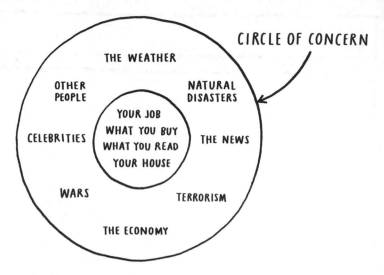

PEOPLE WITH A LARGE CIRCLE OF CONCERN TEND TO WORRY ABOUT
THINGS THAT ARE UNIMPORTANT OR OUT OF THEIR CONTROL.
A LOT OF ENERGY IS WASTED ON THINGS THAT DON'T MATTER.

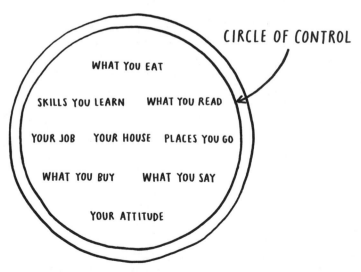

PEOPLE WITH A LARGE CIRCLE OF CONTROL FOCUS THEIR TIME
AND ENERGY ON THINGS THAT ARE WITHIN THEIR CONTROL
(ALTHOUGH THEY PROBABLY STILL WORRY ABOUT OTHER PEOPLE).

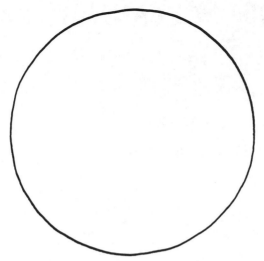

HOW DO YOUR CIRCLES OF CONCERN AND CONTROL LOOK?

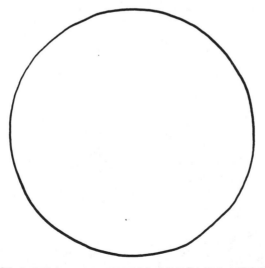

HOW WOULD THEY IDEALLY LOOK?

THINGS YOU CANNOT CHANGE

THINGS YOU CAN CHANGE

LIST SOME NEGATIVE EVENTS YOU'VE HEARD ABOUT IN THE NEWS RECENTLY

LIST AS MANY POSITIVE EVENTS YOU CAN THINK OF THAT YOU'VE HEARD ABOUT IN THE SAME WAY

MAKE A TV SCHEDULE FOR THE NEXT WEEK.
CHOOSE ONLY ONE SHOW FOR EACH DAY THAT
YOU <u>REALLY</u> WANT TO WATCH.

IF THERE ISN'T ONE, LEAVE THAT DAY BLANK.

<u>WATCH ONLY THESE SHOWS.</u>

MONDAY

TUESDAY

WEDNESDAY

THURSDAY

FRIDAY

SATURDAY

SUNDAY

WHEN I GOT MY
FIRST TELEVISION
SET, I STOPPED
CARING SO MUCH
ABOUT CLOSE
RELATIONSHIPS.

ANDY WARHOL

MAKE (OR TAKE) AN IMAGE
THAT REPRESENTS YOU

WHAT ARE THE THREE MAIN
QUALITIES YOU NOTICE?

HOW DOES IT MAKE YOU FEEL?

ASK A FRIEND TO DO THE SAME
(WITHOUT SAYING WHY)

DO YOU SEE THREE
DIFFERENT QUALITIES?

HOW DOES IT MAKE YOU FEEL?

DRAW YOURSELF AS AN EMOJI

THIS IS ME

DRAW THE EMOJI YOU HOPE TO BE

I HOPE TO BE THIS ⟶

SOME THINGS YOU'VE NEVER HAD
(BUT WANT)

SOME THINGS YOU'VE NEVER DONE (BUT WANT TO)

We've somehow become attached to the belief that we should be happy, forever and ever, and that we've failed if we're not. Which is crazy, if you actually think about it. I bought into that belief as much as anyone, and it made me instinctively try to limit any chance of sadness. I would avoid situations and relationships that I thought could end up making me sad. But limiting your sadness doesn't automatically mean you'll be you happy. In fact, sadness often happens as a result of having once been happy. So by limiting your chances of sadness, you're also limiting your chances of happiness.

It's ok to feel happy, and it's ok to feel sad. It's perfectly natural. The same as it's ok to feel angry, or grateful, or jealous, or proud, or... you get the idea. Happiness and sadness are both feelings — neither one is right, and neither one is wrong. The sooner you accept that you cannot protect yourself from sadness, the sooner you will stop protecting yourself from happiness.

YOU CANNOT PROTECT YOURSELF FROM SADNESS WITHOUT PROTECTING YOURSELF FROM HAPPINESS

JONATHAN SAFRAN FOER,
*EXTREMELY LOUD
AND INCREDIBLY CLOSE*

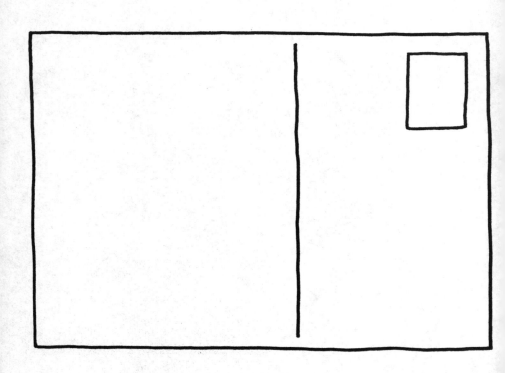

A MESSAGE YOU'LL NEVER SEND

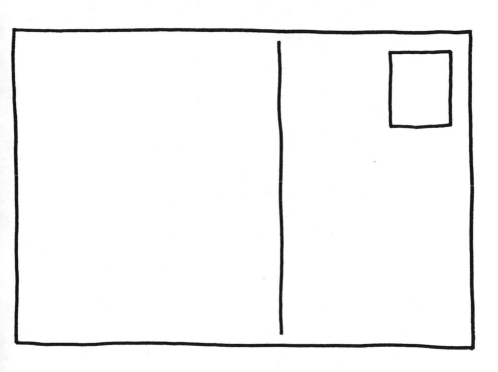

A MESSAGE YOU'LL SEND <u>TODAY</u>

CHOCOLATE MEDITATION
(EATING MINDFULLY)

SIT COMFORTABLY, AWAY FROM DISTRACTIONS.

TAKE A PIECE OF CHOCOLATE IN YOUR HAND.

REALLY LOOK AT IT.

FEEL ITS WEIGHT AND TEXTURE.

LOOK AT ITS COLOR, OR COLORS.

NOTICE HOW YOU ARE DYING
TO SHOVE IT INTO YOUR MOUTH.

DON'T. SMELL IT INSTEAD.

DID YOU KNOW IT SMELLED LIKE THIS?

OK, PUT IT SLOWLY INTO YOUR MOUTH.

LET IT SIT ON YOUR TONGUE.

DOES THE FLAVOR CHANGE AS IT MELTS?

ARE THERE MORE FLAVORS THAN YOU THOUGHT?

HOLD IT IN YOUR MOUTH AS LONG AS YOU CAN.

DOES THIS FEEL WEIRD?

OK. YOU CAN EAT IT.

SPEND THE REST OF YOUR DAY EATING MORE MINDFULLY. DO THIS WITH AT LEAST THREE BITES OF EVERYTHING YOU EAT.

WHAT HAD THE MOST ONE-DIMENSIONAL TASTE?

WHAT HAD MORE FLAVOR THAN YOU REALIZED?

WHAT HAD THE WEIRDEST TEXTURE?

WHAT TASTED BETTER THAN IT USUALLY DOES?

WHICH OF THESE DO YOU RELATE TO?
(ADD MORE OF YOUR OWN)

- [ ] I'M A FAILURE
- [ ] I CAN'T DO ANYTHING
- [ ] NOBODY LIKES ME
- [ ] I'M NOT SMART ENOUGH
- [ ] IT'S BOUND TO GO WRONG
- [ ] WHY BOTHER?
- [ ] NOBODY CARES ABOUT ME
- [ ] CAKE IS A VEGETABLE

DO YOU HAVE ANY HARD EVIDENCE (FACTS) TO SUPPORT THESE FEELINGS?

IT CAN BE EASY TO IMAGINE THAT EVERYTHING
IN LIFE IS EITHER BLACK OR WHITE.

ONE OF TWO EXTREMES.

BUT...

 →LIFE HAPPENS HERE←

FILL THE OPPOSITE PAGE WITH AS MANY
SHADES OF GRAY AS YOU CAN FIND OR CREATE.

REMEMBER THIS PAGE WHEN YOU
ARE THINKING THE BEST, OR WORST.

LET YOUR LIFE BE A LITTLE MORE GRAY.

WHAT EVENT ON THE HORIZON IS MAKING YOU ANXIOUS?

SUM UP WHY IN ONE SENTENCE.

WHAT'S THE WORST THING THAT COULD HAPPEN?

AND THE BEST?

WHAT ABOUT SOMETHING BETWEEN BEST AND WORST?

COME BACK AFTER THE EVENT — WHAT ACTUALLY HAPPENED?

WHICH ANSWER WAS CLOSEST TO THE REALITY?

OK, LET'S TAKE
A FIVE-MINUTE
BREAK, TO SEE
WHAT'S GOING ON
IN YOUR MIND.

FIND A COMFORTABLE POSITION
AWAY FROM ANY DISTRACTIONS.

JUST SIT THERE.

TRY TO NOTICE ANY SENSATIONS
IN YOUR BODY AND MIND.

IF YOUR MIND STARTS TO DRIFT TO YOUR
TO-DO LIST, NOTICE WHERE IT WENT
AND COME BACK TO THE PRESENT.

ARE YOU TENSE?

IS YOUR MIND SPINNING?

ARE YOU IN THE PAST OR FUTURE
RATHER THAN THE PRESENT MOMENT?

DRAW ANY PHYSICAL SENSATIONS YOU FEEL WHEN YOU GET SAD OR ANXIOUS

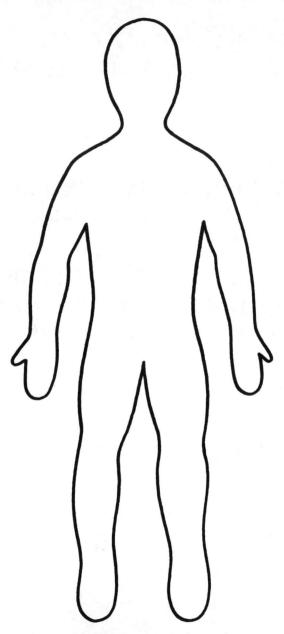

PICK A PREDOMINANT FEELING AND TRACK ITS MOVEMENT THROUGH YOUR BODY

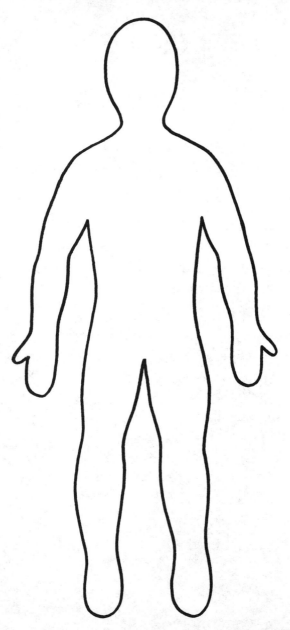

I could probably write a whole different book about getting back that sense of natural curiosity we had as children. It's something that I always tried to retain, and it's something that I always believed was important. I realized just how important it was when I got really sad. I started to lose my curiosity, bit by bit, and as a result I became less interested — first in things and then in life. Everything became desaturated and flat, and not in a cool Instagram filter kind of way.

Being more curious about the world instantly makes you more curious about life. The more questions you ask yourself, the more eager you become to discover the answers, and the more open you are to the world, the more you will make of it. Life is so much more enjoyable when you're interested in living it, and the very first step is strengthening your curiosity.

THE MOST
IMPORTANT EXERCISE
IS STRENGTHENING
YOUR CURIOSITY

TAKE A PHOTO OF SOMETHING THAT YOU NOTICE FOR THE FIRST TIME TODAY.

IT COULD BE THE FLECK OF COLOR IN A FRIEND'S EYES, A SECRET DOORWAY, OR THAT YOU HAVE A REALLY CUTE SMILE.

DO THE SAME FOR THE REST OF THE WEEK

TWO

THREE

FOUR

FIVE

SIX

SEVEN

TAG YOUR PHOTOS #HTBHBOOK
SO WE CAN DISCOVER THEM TOO

LIST FIVE PEOPLE AND HOW YOU THINK THEY'D DESCRIBE YOU IN ONE SENTENCE

NAME	ASSUMED DESCRIPTION OF ME

NOW ASK THEM TO DESCRIBE YOU IN ONE SENTENCE

NAME	ACTUAL DESCRIPTION OF ME

COMMON THINKING DISTORTIONS

Everyone is prone to distortions in thinking, but when you're depressed or anxious these distortions become much more exaggerated. Below is a list of common distorted thinking patterns. Do you recognize yourself in any of them? Once you've noticed that you think in a certain way, it's much easier to limit or stop those thought patterns in the future. (I've drawn a star next to any that apply to me.)

☐ BLACK AND WHITE THINKING*

You think in absolutes, that things are either good or bad, with no middle ground. Practice thinking about the gray areas between the two absolutes. Once you've thought of the best and the worst, what are some in-between options?

☐ CATASTROPHIZING*

You tend to massively exaggerate the importance of events and how terrible they are going to be. Try to put your thoughts in perspective. Things are rarely as important as you let yourself believe, and things rarely go as wrong as you can imagine.

☐ EMOTIONAL REASONING*

You believe your feelings to be hard evidence of the way things are. When you're sad, anxious, or stressed it can give you a warped view of reality. Try to think about the facts of the situation. Do they support your feelings?

☐ FORTUNE TELLING*

You make predictions about things that you have no evidence for, such as how people think, what will happen, or what someone will say to you. You can never predict any of those things, no matter how hard you try. Remind yourself that your guess might — and probably will — be wrong.

(CHECK ANY THAT APPLY TO YOU)

☐ **LABELING**

You attach definite and general labels such as "useless" or "failure" to things that are far too complex to be categorized. Try to avoid using these rigid labels and instead celebrate complexities.

☐ **LIVING BY FIXED RULES***

You tend to live by very rigid statements and use words like "should," "must," and "can't." The more rigid these statements are the more disappointed and angry you will feel. Try to challenge your rigid thinking by using more fluid words such as "wish to," "but," and "would like."

☐ **LOW FRUSTRATION TOLERANCE**

You assume things that are merely annoying are intolerable or unbearable. You exaggerate how bad a situation is and minimize your ability to cope. Try to remind yourself that just because something is annoying it doesn't mean that you can't handle it.

☐ **NEGATIVE FOCUS***

You tend to focus on the negative; ignoring, downplaying, or misinterpreting the positives of a situation. You obsess about your bad points and dismiss your good points. If you do something good, practice celebrating it and accepting the praise and positive feedback.

☐ **PERSONALIZING***

You take responsibility and blame for everything even if it has nothing to do with you. Remind yourself that you are not the center of the universe, and that is a good thing!

FILL THESE BOXES WITH YOUR FREQUENT NEGATIVE THOUGHTS

IF I GET THIS WRONG I MIGHT AS WELL GIVE UP ALTOGETHER. I'M OBVIOUSLY A FAILURE.

LABEL = CATASTROPHIZING

USING THE LIST ON THE PREVIOUS PAGES, LABEL YOUR THOUGHTS WITH THE UNDERLYING THEME

RECORD ANY NEGATIVE TWEET OR STATUS UPDATE YOU THINK OF HERE

USE THIS SPACE TO THINK OF POSITIVE ALTERNATIVES

BORROW AN ALBUM YOU HATE

LISTEN TO IT ALL DAY
(OR AT LEAST FIVE TIMES)

MAKE YOUR OWN VERSION OF THE COVER

WHAT WAS YOUR FAVORITE SONG?

_____

WHAT ARE THE MAIN THREE THEMES?

HOW MANY SONGS DO YOU THINK ARE BASED ON TRUTH?

WHICH LYRICS RESONATED?

_____

_____

_____

HOW DID YOU FEEL
LISTENING TO THE ALBUM?

HOW DO YOU THINK
THE ARTIST FEELS?

I always imagined that I'd be happier when...
when I had a bit more money, when I lived in a
different place, or when I landed a dream job.
But whenever I arrive at one of those "whens"
nothing really changes. I am still the same
person, just in a different situation. It's rare that
external "whens" will ever make you happy.
In the same way that "stuff" rarely makes you
happy — not in any real or lasting sense anyway.

If I asked you to make a list of the things that you
think might make you happy, and a list of things
that actually make you happy, I think you'd find
the second list would be full of things that are
readily available now, not when.

THE THINGS YOU NEED FOR HAPPINESS AREN'T THE THINGS YOU THINK YOU NEED

IRENE MUENI

THINGS THAT YOU THINK WILL MAKE YOU HAPPIER

EVERYTHING THAT YOU KNOW MAKES YOU HAPPY

TAPE A PHOTO HERE THAT MAKES YOU FEEL HAPPIER.

SPEND THE NEXT FEW MINUTES LOOKING AT IT.

REMEMBER THE SCENE AS VIVIDLY AS YOU CAN.

REMEMBER SMALL DETAILS AND BIG FEELINGS.

USING VISUAL ANCHORS IS A GOOD WAY TO BOOST
YOUR MOOD WHEN YOU'RE FEELING LOW.

YOU COULD HANG PHOTOS IN YOUR BEDROOM,
KEEP TRINKETS ON YOUR DESK, AND STORE
A LOVE LETTER IN YOUR BAG.

COLLECT A SERIES OF THINGS THAT MAKE
YOU FEEL GOOD WHEN YOU LOOK AT THEM.

MAKE A LIST OF YOUR VISUAL ANCHORS:

_____

_____

_____

_____

_____

YOU CAN USE ANY OF YOUR SENSES TO BOOST YOUR
MOOD. LIST SOME ANCHORS FOR YOUR OTHER SENSES...

SMELL:

_____

_____

_____

_____

_____

SOUND:

_____

_____

_____

_____

_____

TASTE:

_____

_____

_____

_____

_____

TOUCH:

_____

_____

_____

_____

_____

ALLOW YOURSELF TO BE
LESS THAN PREFECT.

DRAW OR LIST YOUR
"IMPERFECTIONS" ON
THE OPPOSITE PAGE.

SPOILER ALERT: IMPERFECTIONS ARE THE THINGS THAT MAKE YOU YOU.

YOU JUST MADE A LIST OF THINGS TO EMBRACE, CELEBRATE, AND BE PROUD OF.

IF I WERE A _____ I'D BE _____

COLOR:_____

FOOD:_____

DRINK:_____

BOOK:_____

MOVIE:_____

SONG:_____

PIECE OF CLOTHING:_____

VEHICLE:_____

ILLNESS:_____

CARTOON CHARACTER:_____

SOCIAL NETWORK:_____

WEATHER:_____

CITY:_____

SUPERHERO:_____

SUPER-VILLAIN:_____

PLANET:_____

IF I WERE AN ANIMAL, I'D LOOK LIKE THIS:

MAKE A COLLAGE OF WORRIES

MAKE A COLLAGE OF CALM

WHAT'S THE WORST THAT COULD HAPPEN?

DESCRIBE IT IN DETAIL

I found the question opposite in *The Antidote* by Oliver Burkeman, and I've started to ask myself this whenever I feel bad. I haven't been able to answer "yes" once yet, despite asking myself this while I've been curled up on the floor crying my eyes out. I mean, being curled up on the floor crying my eyes out was kind of a problem — but there was no actual problem causing that, if you see what I mean?

Try asking yourself this question next time you're feeling like everything is hopeless. Do you really have a problem right now? If the answer is no, you're probably doing ok, so try to keep going. If the answer is yes, try to work out exactly what the problem is, and then think of ways you could solve it. It's a very effective system.

DO YOU HAVE A PROBLEM RIGHT NOW?

20-MINUTE WORRY WINDOW

CHOOSE A TIME WHEN YOU HAVE 20 MINUTES FREE.

THIS IS YOUR WORRY WINDOW.

WORRY INTENSELY ABOUT EVERYTHING.

MAKE SURE YOU WORRY FOR THE FULL 20 MINUTES.

IF YOU STOP WORRYING BEFORE THE TIME IS UP, YOU SHOULD WORRY ABOUT WHY YOU'RE NOT WORRYING.

SERIOUSLY, THIS IS YOUR ONE CHANCE TO WORRY TODAY.

DO NOT LET YOURSELF WORRY OUTSIDE THIS WINDOW.

IF YOU WORRY ABOUT ANYTHING OUTSIDE THE WINDOW, MAKE A MENTAL NOTE TO WORRY ABOUT IT DURING THE NEXT AVAILABLE WINDOW.

SCRIBBLE, DOODLE, AND DRAW YOUR WORRIES IN THIS WINDOW

SPEND TODAY SEARCHING FOR TINY
DETAILS THAT LOOK LIKE BIG PLACES.

A FLOWER BED COULD BE A JUNGLE,
A CRACK COULD BE A CANYON,
A PEBBLE COULD BE A MOUNTAIN...

PHOTOGRAPH OR DRAW YOUR FAVORITE TINY DETAIL.

WHO OR WHAT LIVES THERE?
IS IT ON EARTH, IN SPACE, OR FANTASY?
DO THEY STILL HAVE PIZZA?

WRITE A STORY (OR DESCRIPTION) ABOUT IT.

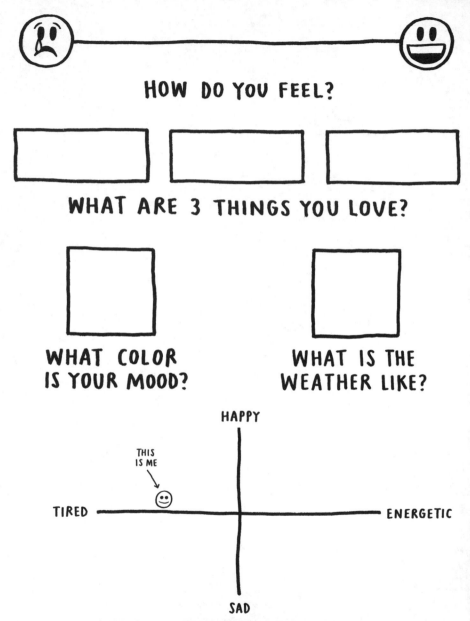

WHERE ARE YOU HEADING?

WHAT SHAPE
IS YOUR LIFE?

WHAT IS THE MOST
IMPORTANT THING?

HOW FULL IS
YOUR MIND?

HOW FULL IS
YOUR HEART?

WHEN WAS THE LAST TIME YOU WERE HAPPY?

WHICH AREAS ARE IMPROVING, WHICH ARE GETTING WORSE?
ARE YOU DRINKING ENOUGH WATER?

OVERALL MOOD: 1 2 3 4 5 6 7 8 9 10

FAMILY: 1 2 3 4 5 6 7 8 9 10

FRIENDS: 1 2 3 4 5 6 7 8 9 10

SOCIAL LIFE: 1 2 3 4 5 6 7 8 9 10

RELATIONSHIP: 1 2 3 4 5 6 7 8 9 10

HAVING FUN: 1 2 3 4 5 6 7 8 9 10

WORK: 1 2 3 4 5 6 7 8 9 10

MONEY: 1 2 3 4 5 6 7 8 9 10

EATING HEALTHY: 1 2 3 4 5 6 7 8 9 10

DRINKING WATER: 1 2 3 4 5 6 7 8 9 10

GOING OUTSIDE: 1 2 3 4 5 6 7 8 9 10

EXERCISE (UGH): 1 2 3 4 5 6 7 8 9 10

HEALTH: 1 2 3 4 5 6 7 8 9 10

CREATIVITY: 1 2 3 4 5 6 7 8 9 10

SENSE OF PURPOSE: 1 2 3 4 5 6 7 8 9 10

THE PAST: 1 2 3 4 5 6 7 8 9 10

THE PRESENT: 1 2 3 4 5 6 7 8 9 10

THE FUTURE: 1 2 3 4 5 6 7 8 9 10

CLOSE YOUR EYES FOR FIVE MINUTES AND CONCENTRATE ON LISTENING.

IF YOUR MIND STARTS TO WANDER, MAKE A MENTAL NOTE OF THE THOUGHT AND COME BACK TO THE SOUNDS.

PAY ATTENTION TO EVERY LITTLE NOISE.

WHAT DO YOU THINK MADE THOSE SOUNDS?

THE LOUDEST

THE QUIETEST

THE MOST ORDINARY

THE MOST UNUSUAL

IMAGINE YOU ARE 90 YEARS OLD.

I WISH I HAD SPENT MORE TIME ON

○

○

○

REFLECT ON YOUR LIFE IN THESE TWO LISTS.

I WISH I HAD SPENT LESS TIME ON

When I get really down I have a tendency to start doing everything on autopilot — I'm doing something, but I'm not really there. The more sad I get, the less present I am. I become trapped worrying about the future, or dwelling on the past. Last year I spent most of my time doing things without even noticing. I self-diagnosed myself with anhedonia* more times than I can remember. I think I did experience anhedonia to some extent — I was unable to take pleasure in life — but that's because I was rarely completely present in life.

I have since tried to be more intentional in everything I do. Which simply means I've slowed down a bit and started paying more attention to things again. I'm actually trying to do things that I want to do, and notice when I'm doing them. That can be much harder than it sounds, especially when you're sad. But the more you do it, the more natural it becomes — and the only way you'll ever experience happiness is by actually being present when you feel it.

* The inability to feel pleasure in normally pleasurable activities.

DO LESS
BE MORE

CARRIE CONTEY PhD

DESIGN SOME AWARDS TO CELEBRATE YOU!

THEY CAN BE FOR YOUR BIGGEST
ACHIEVEMENTS OR SMALLEST VICTORIES

SOME IDEAS:
YOUR BEST QUALITY
YOUR FAVORITE FEATURE
THAT THING YOU DO BEST

LISTEN TO THE SADDEST SONG YOU KNOW

NOW PLAYING...

MENU

LISTEN TO IT A FEW TIMES.
WALLOW IN THE LYRICS.
SOAK IN HOW THE ARTIST FEELS.

HOW DO YOU FEEL?

NOW DO THE SAME WITH THE HAPPIEST SONG

SING ALONG AS LOUDLY AS YOU CAN.
DANCE AROUND LIKE AN IDIOT.
IMAGINE THIS SONG IS ALL THERE IS.

DO YOU FEEL BETTER?

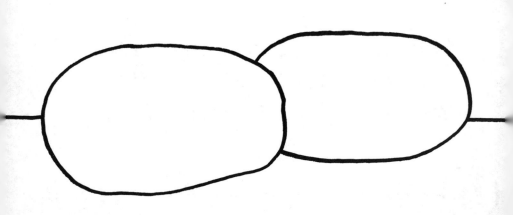

DECORATE A LARGE PEBBLE OR ROCK.

LEAVE IT SOMEWHERE VISIBLE IN PUBLIC.

YOU HAVE JUST MADE THE WORLD A HAPPIER PLACE.

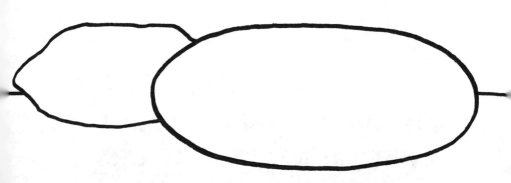

PRACTICE YOUR DESIGNS ON THESE PEBBLES.

LIVE TODAY AS IF YOU
ARE NEW TO THIS PLANET.

LOOK AT EVERYTHING
WITH A FRESH CURIOSITY.

CONSTANTLY ASK YOURSELF <u>WHY.</u>

WHY IS YOUR COFFEE BROWN?
WHY DON'T STRANGERS SAY HELLO?
WHY DO NEWSPAPERS EXIST?
WHY DOES BAD FOOD TASTE SO GOOD?

WHICH ORDINARY THING
NOW SEEMS STRANGER?

WHAT SHOULD HUMANS
DO DIFFERENTLY?

WHAT WAS THE MAIN
NGREDIENT IN YOUR FOOD?

DRAW A GRAPH OF
SOCIETY'S MOOD

SET SOME ALARMS FOR RANDOM
TIMES THROUGHOUT THE DAY.

WHENEVER AN ALARM SOUNDS,
STOP FOR A FEW MINUTES.

NOTICE WHAT'S GOING ON IN
YOUR MIND AND BODY.

THAT'S IT.

10:14 AM

HEY, WHAT ARE
YOU THINKING?

11:11 AM

WHAT ARE YOU
WISHING FOR?

2:07 PM

ARE YOU LOST
IN THOUGHT?

4:19 PM

REMEMBER, YOU
ARE NOT YOUR
THOUGHTS.

IMPROVISE YOUR DAY

CHOOSE A DAY WHEN YOU HAVE NO PLANS.
MAKE IT UP AS YOU GO. <u>DON'T STAY INSIDE!</u>

SOME SUGGESTIONS:
TREAT YOUR MOM TO LUNCH.
VISIT A LOCAL TOURIST SPOT.
TAKE A RANDOM BUS OR TRAIN.
WALK THE LENGTH OF YOUR CITY.
ONLY TURN LEFT.

WHERE DID YOU GO AND WHAT DID YOU DO?

The internet is arguably humanity's second greatest invention, after the cheeseburger. It has the potential to give you the answer to any question, connect you to any person, and make you laugh out loud (LOL!) in seconds. But it's also made it so much easier to compare yourself with other people — other people who appear to be doing better than you. It's important to remember that they are editing their lives for public consumption, just like you. Comparing the private realities of your life with the public highlights of everyone else's life is a really bad idea. But I know how easy it can be to do that, and how hard it can be to stop.

That's where being more intentional helped me again. I turned off all of my social media notifications, and I deleted my Facebook account. I've not regretted doing either of those things, but I'm not suggesting that you need to do something quite so drastic. The main change I made was quite a small one — I now only check social media when I want to, rather than when it beeps at me, or when I'm bored or procrastinating. It's really hard to stop comparing yourself to other people, especially when everyone's life is streaming right in front of your eyes. But choosing when you dip into that stream is a good start.

DON'T COMPARE YOUR INSIDES WITH SOMEONE ELSE'S OUTSIDES

SPEND A DAY WITH NO INTERNET

IT MAY HELP TO FIND ANALOG
VERSIONS OF THE INTERNET

AMAZON = VISIT THE MALL

GOOGLE = GO TO THE LIBRARY

INSTAGRAM = GO OUTDOORS (OR EAT LUNCH)

TUMBLR = VISIT AN ART GALLERY

TWITTER = LISTEN TO STRANGERS MOANING

WHERE DID YOU GO?

WHAT DID YOU MISS?

WHAT WAS THE HIGHLIGHT?

HOW MANY EMAILS
DID YOU GET?

HOW MANY WERE
IMPORTANT?

HOW DO
YOU FEEL?

OK, HOW MANY TIMES DID YOU CAVE IN?

SMALL THINGS

BIG THINGS

WALK BAREFOOT ON THE GRASS.

NOTICE THE SENSATIONS.

HOW DO THEY DIFFER FROM WALKING IN SHOES?

IS ANYONE ELSE BAREFOOT?

IS ANYONE LOOKING AT YOU FUNNY?

SMILE AT ALL OF THEM (NOT IN A CREEPY WAY).

HOW LONG DID THE GRASS FEEL?

WHAT NON-GRASS PLANTS WERE ON THE GROUND?

HOW DID YOU FEEL

BEFORE?   DURING?   AFTER?

TURN BACK A RANDOM NUMBER OF
PAGES AND ANALYZE YOUR ANSWER.

IF THERE IS NO TASK ON THAT PAGE,
TURN TO THE NEXT COMPLETED TASK.

HOW DO YOU FEEL LOOKING AT YOUR ANSWER?

HOW DO YOU THINK YOU FELT THEN?

CAN YOU LEARN ANYTHING FROM
YOUR ANSWER ON THAT PAGE?

GO TO THE CINEMA AND WATCH A MOVIE YOU WOULD NOT ORDINARILY CHOOSE

WHAT DID YOU SEE?

WHAT DID YOU EAT?

HOW WAS IT?

WHAT WAS THE OVERALL MESSAGE OR MORAL?

THINK OF THE ONE THING YOU ARE
REALLY DWELLING ON AT THE MOMENT.

THE THING YOU WANT
TO LET GO OF FOREVER.

WRITE THAT THING ON A CARD.

BUY A HELIUM-FILLED BALLOON.

ATTACH THAT THING TO THE STRING.

LET GO.

ONE LAST TIME. ARE THINGS GETTING BETTER?

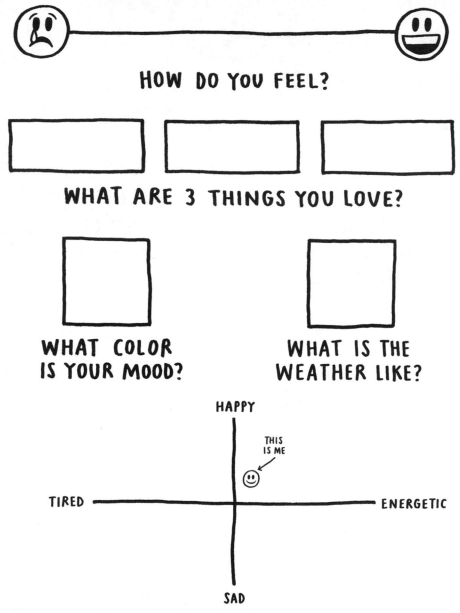

HOW DO YOU FEEL?

WHAT ARE 3 THINGS YOU LOVE?

WHAT COLOR
IS YOUR MOOD?

WHAT IS THE
WEATHER LIKE?

HAPPY

THIS
IS ME

TIRED

ENERGETIC

SAD

WHERE ARE YOU ON THIS SCALE?

WHERE ARE YOU HEADING?

WHAT SHAPE
IS YOUR LIFE?

WHAT IS THE MOST
IMPORTANT THING?

HOW FULL IS
YOUR MIND?

HOW FULL IS
YOUR HEART?

WHEN WAS THE LAST TIME YOU WERE HAPPY?

WHICH AREAS ARE IMPROVING, WHICH ARE GETTING WORSE?
REMEMBER TO MAKE TIME FOR FUN.

OVERALL MOOD: 1 2 3 4 5 6 7 8 9 10
FAMILY: 1 2 3 4 5 6 7 8 9 10
FRIENDS: 1 2 3 4 5 6 7 8 9 10
SOCIAL LIFE: 1 2 3 4 5 6 7 8 9 10
RELATIONSHIP: 1 2 3 4 5 6 7 8 9 10
HAVING FUN: 1 2 3 4 5 6 7 8 9 10
WORK: 1 2 3 4 5 6 7 8 9 10
MONEY: 1 2 3 4 5 6 7 8 9 10
EATING HEALTHY: 1 2 3 4 5 6 7 8 9 10
DRINKING WATER: 1 2 3 4 5 6 7 8 9 10
GOING OUTSIDE: 1 2 3 4 5 6 7 8 9 10
EXERCISE (UGH): 1 2 3 4 5 6 7 8 9 10
HEALTH: 1 2 3 4 5 6 7 8 9 10
CREATIVITY: 1 2 3 4 5 6 7 8 9 10
SENSE OF PURPOSE: 1 2 3 4 5 6 7 8 9 10
THE PAST: 1 2 3 4 5 6 7 8 9 10
THE PRESENT: 1 2 3 4 5 6 7 8 9 10
THE FUTURE: 1 2 3 4 5 6 7 8 9 10

IT'S OK TO GET HELP

There are many organizations out there to help you when you're feeling sad, anxious, or worse.

They vary from country to country, so I've made a list that I will try to keep updated at HAPPYLIST.LEECRUTCHLEY.COM

If you need someone to talk to right now:

You can chat with someone via IM at IMALIVE.ORG

And you can email The Samaritans at JO@SAMARITANS.ORG

WHAT NOW?

A big problem with self-help books is that when you get to the end, it feels like an end. You may know what you should do, according to the author, but essentially you still feel the same. I always intended this book to help you discover and remember a few things that make you feel happier, rather than tell you what I think will make you happier. Because I really have no idea. So please don't treat the end of this book like it's an end for you. Because as corny and "self-help" as it sounds, this is a beginning, if you want it to be.

Obviously there will still be times when you sink into sadness. Life is unpredictable, and shit has the habit of happening. In fact — even though I feel much better on the whole — I'm writing this exactly two days after crying for hours, uncontrollably and for no reason. It came out of nowhere, when it felt like everything was going pretty great. That reminded me how important momentum and effort are when it comes to feeling less sad. I'd let slip all of the things that made me feel better. I felt so much happier that I got lazy about it. I thought I didn't need to try anymore. But it's obvious that I did, do, and will need to keep trying — and so will you.

The thing that is different these days is that I feel better equipped to cope with those dark times. I have a list of things that I know will actually help me, and as soon as I'm ready to try, I will start to feel less sad again. I hope you've discovered a similar list, and I hope you continue to remind yourself of it every day. It may not be that easy to BE HAPPY, but you know that it's possible to feel a bit less sad.

WRITE YOUR "LESS SAD" LIST ON THIS PAGE

NEVER FORGET IT

RECOMMENDED READING

NAÏVE. SUPER. — ERLEND LOE

THE ANTIDOTE — OLIVER BURKEMAN

WHY ARE YOU SO SAD? — JASON PORTER

MOTHER. WIFE. SISTER. HUMAN. WARRIOR. FALCON.
YARDSTICK. TURBAN. CABBAGE. — ROB DELANEY

MINDFULNESS — MARK WILLIAMS AND DANNY PENMAN

WHAT'S STOPPING YOU? — ROBERT KELSEY

SANE NEW WORLD — RUBY WAX

IT'S KIND OF A FUNNY STORY — NED VIZZINI

HYPERBOLE AND A HALF — ALLIE BROSH

AND I URGE

NOTICE WHEN

AND EXCLAIM OR

AT SOME POINT,

NICE, I DON'T

YOU TO PLEASE
YOU ARE HAPPY,
MURMUR OR THINK
'IF THIS ISN'T
KNOW WHAT IS."

KURT VONNEGUT,
A MAN WITHOUT A COUNTRY

THANK YOU

As always, to my family and friends. It feels stupid and obvious to thank them in each book I write. But, while I'm writing each book, I'm reminded just how important they are, and where I would be without them.

To my editor, Marian Lizzi, and the team at Perigee for continuing to believe in my ideas enough to publish them.

To Oliver Burkeman for adding his words to this book, and for writing a book that didn't promise to change my life — but kind of did.

To everyone who believed in this book enough to endorse it. Your work and words have helped me more than you realize.

And to anyone else who has ever made, said, or sang something real and honest. You probably don't know it, but you keep people going.

ABOUT THE AUTHOR

Lee Crutchley is a tall human from a small town in England. He is an artist and author, and this book you are holding is his third. His others are *Quoteskine Volume 1* and *The Art of Getting Started*. He is writing this in the third person, which feels both right and wrong.

He has a website: **LEECRUTCHLEY.COM**

He is social: **@LEECRUTCHLEY**

© Jayne Yong

THINGS TO REMEMBER

1. IT'S OK TO FEEL HAPPY
2. IT'S OK TO FEEL SAD